Via Storm Clouds

Collected Poetry

by Leghorn Faust

authorHOUSE®

AuthorHouse™
1663 Liberty Drive
Bloomington, IN 47403
www.authorhouse.com
Phone: 1 (800) 839-8640

Cover Image by: Brittany Vandegraft

Published by AuthorHouse 09/22/2016

ISBN: 978-1-5246-0011-2 (sc)
ISBN: 978-1-5246-0012-9 (e)

Print information available on the last page.

Someday this book will be dedicated to someone

Via Storm Clouds

Celeste

someone
a girl
once told me
"Your problem
is that you know
what you want."

I wasn't paying attention
to what she was telling me
though
I was too busy
watching her clothes
ride the curves of her body

Somewhere, Everywhere

she's like rock and roll
but she don't look it
to tell
you'd have to look
into her bloodshot eyes

staying up with her all night
reading in bed
books by David Sedaris
while she laid quietly
hallucinating to herself
and singing songs
about Jesus Christ in her head
careful, not to offend
proving that the only thing
a girl can do wrong
is not be herself

we didn't always have to get naked
in order to have a good time

on those most memorable of occasions
we'd just stay up and talk or argue
about faith, science, rationality and reason
as well as the history of ignorance
death, dying, the earth
with its continuously
shifting tectonic plates
proving once again, that the earth

is just a slight bit older than 6,000 years
and that anyone who will tell you otherwise
has a religious agenda

patience, impatience,
the time I got ran over by a car
provocative album covers
and the great works of the Amish,
with their furniture

together, her and I would prove
over and over again
that such close friends of the opposite sex
didn't always have to get naked
in order to have a great evening in bed

though it does help sometimes

Insensibilities and A Lack Of Discretion

the people were reading,
combing, texting, writing,
listening to their favorite bands,
heating coffee beans
and smacking the scoops
against the knock box
as music played over the speakers

but no one was paying attention
to any of that in particular

they were all too self-involved
in what they were discussing
as a woman said how tired
she was of having to download
music onto her computer

the guy working the cash register
did his best to explain
to a girl who had never been there before
about the differences between
slow drip and French press
as a girl with a pierced nose
and a butt hiked up too high
in the jeans she was wearing
spoke to a man in a business suit
who looked out of place
standing in line next to an elderly man
in a wheelchair and a kid with dreads

the kid in dreads would deliberately
go out of his way to dress
in a grungier fashion than what
he was accustomed to
on account of his parents owning
a house in Orland Park
and sending him to
a high class private school
in central Illinois
which shall remain nameless

as the girl with the hiked up butt
had graduated to discussing how
nude bicycling was looked down upon
and not allowed in the immediate area
to a young man in a tie and sweater
who was less interested
in her predicament
and more in how he thought
she had total First World problems
and perhaps she should
spend some time in the Third World
scrounging around
dumpsters and battlefields
looking for food for a week
just so she could see
how hard she didn't have it

but this was the type of crowd
drawn to these places
stubborn and ill advised

and never wanting to make sure
they made their next thought
without the implementation
of a coffee bean

We Never Made It to 505

he looked at the first text
she had sent
dated September 23, 2012
and the last
on February 7, 2013

and as he baked the pizza
he wondered how she could
change the way she felt
towards him so abruptly
especially with how affectionate
she had been in the beginning
and how they simply carried on

how when she had to pick her stuff
up from an abusive ex's house
he was there to tell her
that she didn't have anything
to fear anymore

or when her mother
said she hadn't amounted
to much in life
he was there to say
that she needn't go back
that the leaves would
still be there in the morning
and to take a stand for herself
and when he finally did meet her mom

she asked "What have you done to my daughter?"

while looking at the messages they shared
he received a new one from a friend
saying how it was still early
and there was a girl he had met at the bar
and how sure he was that she had friends
who were looking for a little company

he responded
"Sure, just let me get cleaned up."
as he turned off the oven, and,
accepting his fate
went upstairs to change
hoping that this night
he would meet a girl
whose text messages
would rival hers

Mutual Reimbursement

the funk music played
she called it her sleepy time music

normally, it would lull her to sleep
but tonight was a special occasion
their first Thanksgiving together
and they were staying up late

he sat perched on her butt
giving her a back massage
it wasn't infrequent
that he'd press down
and hear an immediate crack

she liked it
the scratching, rubbing, kneading,
the faint feel of his fingertips
as they traversed her back
in spirals

when it was his turn
she asked how he got the scars
on his back
he said he honestly
didn't know
they had been there
for as long as he could remember

she said they were beautiful

and started to kiss them
one by one
and when she was done
she laid on top of him
her body slowly rising
with each of his breaths

and feeling her heartbeat
on his back
he turned to her and smiled
"When do I get my back massaged?"

Noir

I was sitting there
by the fish tank
with my big hair
it always used to be so big
with the what not

the party was pretty lame

but she was standing there
sipping on a drink
with the what have you
and influenced entirely
by hallucinogenic drugs

she was completely spaced out
with a faint sweat
above her brow
resembling the kind of sweat
you get while having
frenzied, uncompromising,
lover-pulling-the-back-of-your-head-
by-the-hair type sex

but on this night
her sweat was entirely due
to her being mentally spacious
and out someplace else

I got up to make my move

her figure was
and as I would find out later
always
clad in black
she drowned herself in it
to her
there were no other colors

her eyes widened
when she noticed
the guy with the big hair
making his way toward her

she set down her drink
to put her fingers on her temples
and shouted
"My God! Your hair! I love it!"
before hugging me

and again
as I found out later
the more I was around her
the more I discovered
it wasn't the drugs
she was continuously high on
that made her so sweet

I don't remember much else
of that night
except that we hit it off
and the next day at work

she came in to visit
with a homemade lunch
and that she sat with me
on my break

Going Back to How We Were

they never argued
though she didn't like
how she felt he knew
everything there was
to know about himself

it was intimidating

and he never
knew he played
the part of actor
he certainly
never felt that way

it was something
not worth
talking about

in the end
all she wanted
was for him
to leave
and this reasoning
gave her the perfect excuse
for an out

but he didn't think that

he knew their paths

would cross again
as they always did

and just as they always did
he knew
she would look at him
the way
she was always meant to

Ambigua

the room was
blanketed with heat
he hated summer
and all its troubles
and the wine
wasn’t helping
so he left

it was still
early enough
that a coffeehouse
would be open

he went through the names
in his phone
of all the people
he didn’t want
to call
only to find
out that no one
was already
waiting there

so he sat in a corner
with his laptop

when the barista
called his drink
that was the last time

he would move
for the next three hours
not typing a word

when the coffeehouse closed
the girl
who had been playing guitar
made small talk as he left

proving to him, irrevocably,
for the time being at least
that he had
enough material
for yet another poem

and that should he go home
he hoped
to get it typed
before going
to bed

Debutante

compliments can be empty, merciless
especially when you're working
as assistant manager
at some minor coffee shop

while your friend struggles
with his own hazardous sort of existence
somewhere, far away,
that is, like another state

content with his hermit-like existence
chasing girls that surely,
he will never know
in the somewhere or something
that all along and together again
make up those subtle cities
in Chicago, Illinois

and coffee shop owners
that hate democracy
and freedom of speech
pretend with their conspiracy theories
and non-existent media liberal bias

attack the messenger

those who can't get laid, hate

and don't be surprised

if the first thing she does
when she wakes
is light up that cigarette
she'll never part
with those fags

Ghosts All

supposedly
there was a ghost
that followed the piece
of wood around

it was a piece from
a grand piano
and the name
of the manufacturer
was engraved
on the gold plate
that was
attached to it

this was the
second ghost
to haunt their house
the other being
a girl they could
hear in the basement

or that's what they
told people
when they were over

the sounds
were actually coming
from a radio
that was always

tucked away
in the crawlspace

his roommate
had come up with the idea
thinking it would make
a good conversation piece

much the same
as all the other old relics
in their house did

their VHS tapes
and campaign posters
from United State's Senate races
from the 1890s

their house was a dead zone
from modern pop culture
they didn't know
what anyone
spoke of
in those regards

but it was
a gathering place
for the eccentrics
on Saturday nights
who could brave
the piece of wood
and the radio
that was always on
in the crawlspace

Late Night Birthday Gifts

October 29th, her birthday
but she was at home
she'd had a bad day
and was in no mood
for celebrating

he had called her to see
if he could come over
she said maybe
tomorrow night
and when he pressed
what was wrong
she said she didn't
want to talk about it

he said he at least
wanted to stop by
and give her
her gifts

when she finally relented
he said he'd be there
around nine thirty

when he pulled into her driveway
she was already waiting there
and when he got out from his truck
he handed her a gift bag
with a cross necklace

and two of her favorite
books inside

she knew he wasn't religious
but this wasn't about him
it was about her
it was something she wasn't used to

he held her and asked
if there was anything he could do

she said he was doing it
just by being there
and that she really wanted him to stay
but that she needed
this night for herself

he said alright
and to give him a call
should she need anything
she said she would
and kissed him good night

as he was driving home
she texted him about the necklace
saying she had just put it on
with no intention
of taking it off

Escapade

I've never understood bars myself
at the most
they always seemed an inconvenience

unless there was a poetry reading
to attend

the people
always standing there
talking over each other
as the music plays too loudly
on the jukebox

or worse
someone sings karaoke

and the girls
with their makeup
and unapproachable smiles
wearing black shirts and blue jeans
and how they'll accept a drink from a guy
that they'll work for the evening
and whom they'll thankfully lose
in the men's bathroom
at two in the morning
when he passes out on the floor
and the bartender
will go in to retrieve him
just before the bar closes

at five

that's the most fun
I've ever had
in a bar

not the passing out part
but helping a willowy brunette waitress
carry a drunk out of the bathroom

and hear her tell his friends
that if they want to stay
they'll have to learn to not punch walls
in the bathroom stalls
while releasing their bowels
atop the porcelain bowls

we smoked outside afterwards
the waitress and I
and I gained a whole new appreciation
for the female psyche

that she didn't have time for any
misunderstandings
and had never been with a man
who had hit her

I told her that I never would
hit her that is
and that I lived up the street;
she should pay a visit

when she got off work

I said to just follow the street lamps

she smiled
and said that sometimes
the only thing better than commanding
a room full of drunken men
was the chance to turn down
to tell the most beautiful one
that he was the reason for the sun
coming up in the morning

we talked often after that
anytime I went to the bar

later, she would say
how she pictured being with me
anytime she was with her boyfriend

and I thought to myself "*What a woman*."

Great Afternoon at the Publishing Company

the computer systems
at work crash
giving everyone
an afternoon break

I take an extra hour for my lunch
while the kid I sit next to
talks to the cute brunette
over in sales

he won't miss a thing
making book covers for awhile

when I come back
the systems are still down
and the proofers
are celebrating
by having a smoke
outside

I go into the break room
to read a newspaper
and am confronted
with some horrible news:
"Satirical Novelist
Kurt Vonnegut dies
at the age of 84."

"I guess it's up to me now,"

I think while cutting out
the article

I'm twenty four with one book to my name

this job is nice
it's the first one I've had
where the pay is practical

and the days
I can handle
even when conveniences
such as computer systems crashing
don't fall into my lap

just sitting here
ten hours a day
for a three day weekend
listening to the sound
of fingers, punching keys
on a keyboard

She Must Probably Know A Lot

she must probably
know a lot
what with the way she lets
the smoke settle
in her throat and lungs
before exhaling
or how she'll watch
the way cars
back into each other
while parallel parking

but you'll know
something must be wrong
when she adds
another empty wine bottle
to her collection in the kitchen
or when she'll twitch at the prick
of a tattoo gun
normally, she praises it as being
one of the most pleasant of sensations

but you'll know
something must be right
when he's breaking up
bar room brawls
at three in the morning
what with his not bothering
to wait for the bouncers
to get involved

or how he'll go back
for another drink
and be greeted by a girl
who turned him down
several years back
by saying
that she wanted
to be left alone

or how he'll finally give
her that chance
by privately thinking
that she is every bit
as memorable as
the toilet paper left strewn
about the men's bathroom floor
before turning her down
and telling her
that he has more
important things
on his mind

as he'll reach for a napkin
and request another drink
and think to himself
"One more bottle, one more poem."

None of the Women You Want to be Around

the pseudo feminists
were all there
the type who say
they want respect
but get upset
when a guy
won't mistreat them

they didn't know
they were like this
the same way that
most people don't know
they are the way
they are

and that made the events
all the more pallid

two of them were talking
to a guy he knew to be
a serial abuser
per his ex-girlfriend

it always seemed
that those who
preached self-respect
were those less inclined
to practice

and it was a hypocrisy
that bothered him

where could he begin to find
the type of girl he'd be interested in
if this was all there was?

chewing his last bite of food
and getting up to pay
he thought that if he did
have a chance
then it wouldn't be here
and it wouldn't be tonight

Decalogue of Fire & Water

surrounded by
red and blue curtains
he stood in the shower
thinking of places
he'd rather be

namely the shower
back at her place

he remembered their
days off together
and how they'd gather candles
in her bathroom
and light them

they'd refer to her sink
as their little alter

and as the water ran
he would hold back the curtain
as she stepped in
and let the water collide
then run down her body

he liked seeing her like that
before stepping in himself
and marveling at the way
her hair was already matted
to her head

there they would stand
bathing and holding each other
with hands running down
wet bodies
and locking in and around
wet orifices

"water, liquids, fluids. . . ,"
they would smile
as they mocked
what a strange woman
with a lisp
had mumbled
after playing her set
at a concert
they had been to
a few months back
before returning
to how they had been before

searching, pioneering, exploring

this is how they preferred to be

with him on his knees
cleaning her lower limbs
and letting the soap
and water run into his eyes

and her using her mouth
to clean him

instead of the soap
and wash rag that hung
from the shower wall

and when they finished
they would turn the water off
still holding each other
as the heat escaped the room
but never their bodies

he missed that feeling, that sensation
and wondered
who she was
doing this with now

Femalia

she's the sex fueled tattoo addict
with muscular legs

when she has them wrapped around you
it's like a Chinese finger trap

she has a tattoo of a guillotine
across the small of her back

what's going through it is pure symbolism
a penis getting its head chopped off

this girl's vagina has teeth

Bookend

he went out for a cigarette
it was an okay night
the people there
helped to take his mind
off things

as he lit up
a disheveled woman
approached
"I need a dollar,"
she commanded
it was something
he was used
to hearing
in Saint Louis
and Chicago
but not here

he was going to say
he didn't have a dollar
but before he was even
finished saying no
the woman was
across the street
already stalking
her next victim

when he went
to a coffeehouse

that following Sunday
he again
went outside
for a cigarette

this time
a man shouted at him
from across the street

and as the man
approached
he could see
it was actually
the same woman
from that other night
still needing money

this time it was seventy five cents

"I don't have any money,"
he said

"You never have any money!"
she scolded
and ran up to a girl
who wasn't having any of it
and ignored the woman
by simply walking
into the coffeehouse

Manumit

they sat across from each other
at the coffeehouse
and never ordered food
when the waitress asked
he only ordered for himself a cup of coffee
while she struggled to not want a cigarette
she had kicked the habit
several months ago

it was never what they said to one another
but what they didn't
they had a way of reading one another
just by looking
at each other's facial expressions

but this was the first time
he had seen her in months
and he could tell
that something between the two of them
had changed
she didn't make him feel
the way she used to
and he noticed
that she wore her hair down
to the point where it was almost covering
her entire face . . .

. . . her beautiful face . . .

and for her part
she had noticed certain things about him
had changed too
he was thinner
his mannerisms were different
he didn't say or repeat specific words in his
sentences anymore
like the words "but, uh . . . ,"
to which she would imitate a hi-hat
getting hit
every time he said that

and he didn't look at her
the same way anymore . . .

. . . things had definitely changed . . .

Defecation

go ahead and lie about sex
stupid kid at the picnic park bench
I'm sure that all the people
and their thumbs
are quite impressed
with the amount of girls you haven't laid

I'm also really glad
that your asshole Republican grandfather
had a seat
on the Illinois Supreme Court
it just makes my voting Democratic
all the much easier

and I can tell by the attitude you wear
that your parents paid handsomely
to have you sent to a private school
gee, golly, gosh and darn
I am so jealous by how much of an ass
your education has made you

I'd also like to say
that we're going bowling tonight
and that you're not invited

I am also
not considering you for the coffee shop job
should I become the assistant manager
you lying, dickless, little flake

Jamaican 45

the bass pounded through the walls
as we sat there watching cop shows
from the nineteen seventies

I could hear my roommate
singing the lyrics
about being a proud black man,
even though he is white

"Do you guys listen to anything
else other than ska music in this house?"
she asked as she creased the page
of her book and set it by her side

she was ready for bed

"Not if we don't have to,"
I said, getting up to play
an old Jamaican 45
in my record player
before coming back to join her

"I still can't believe you're putting
on that show," she said
as we were taken back
to Studio One
where the song I was playing
had been recorded

"Neither can I," I confessed
hoping that I had enough
to pay the three bands
one of whom was reuniting
and hadn't played together in years

I wanted to bury my face
in her breasts
but my energy was sapped
it had taken everything in me
just to get her back home
from the bar the night before

"What are you thinking of?" she asked,
kissing me after I had closed my eyes

"Nothing," I answered honestly,
this whole keeping as busy
as possible thing being new to me

"Are you thinking of her?" she asked,
just as the trumpet and trombone
joined the tenor sax in the chorus

"No," I shrugged,
"Are you thinking of him?"

"Never." She paused, waiting for the song
to return to its verse
"I like this music."

"That's why I listen to it."

"Is that why you're with me?"
there was a tremble to her voice
"Because you like me?"

I opened my eyes to see the faint smile
of the single most acceptable woman
I could have
at the moment
but not the face of the girl
I had fallen for seven years ago

"You know I do."

"No, you don't," she turned away
"You just want to feel something
around all sides of you for the night."

and we waited
until the 45 had finished playing
to turn off the TV
and went to sleep

Aplomb

he sat and looked
and realized
how he had little
in common with others
other than carbon atoms
but with the way the wine tasted
and how it went down
he wondered
if the guy she was with
right now went
that easily into her

but he did have his pens
and notebooks and cigarettes
and the time to get it all down
the time that others wanted
but never allowed themselves to have

a place to go and conquer
what would keep them up at night
to achieve a little immortality
if you will

he never wanted that
he just wanted a way
to live
and the word provided that

he didn't feel so bad

after having that thought
he didn't have much
but he had enough
to know that he had
a certain amount of self-respect
not provided to the other people
sitting around him
at the bar

Freedom Fighter

(Meaning One Who Hates and Fights
Against the Advancement of Freedom)

at one point in my life
my religious fundamentalist boss
at the bookstore where I worked
told me that if it were up to her
she would burn
all the pornographic magazines
and New Age religion books
in the store

I think that is such a funny
and ironic sort of thing
at one point in history
Christianity was also such an echo
of the whole "New Age" movement

not that any "New Age" religion
has had any more impact
or is much better than Christianity
just ask any practitioner
of recent knowledge
and you'll be told that religion is all just
"silly," "hoopla," "harmful,"
"HARMFUL"
and justly so

those who believe less and know more

are more inclined
to carry out a more peaceful
and lucrative existence
and are less likely to hold a grudge
or hurt somebody
than those who think ignorance is a virtue
waiting to be rewarded in death

I did tell my boss
that I thought it was great
that she was such a proud enemy
of the First Amendment

I called her a "fascist" after that
because I couldn't think of anything else
more original and less cliché
but perhaps when she stops being a cliché
is when I'll stop calling her one

Thumbing Through Words

she liked
the idea of him
as opposed
to the real thing

his words
the way he
would portray incidents
on the printed page

this is what
she preferred
as opposed
to his being there
in her living room
her shower
her bed

it was always
so much safer
being apart
as opposed to being
together

that's when she
didn't have to worry
about her routine
being interrupted

her tattoos
her sleeping pills
her nights of waking up
only to feel blood gathering
between her thighs

this never seemed to happen
when he was around

his cooking, cleaning
how he'd take care
of her dog
when she was gone
his willingness to listen
to her
or the way he would
come home
at night
and bask
in the lights
of her small house
as he pulled
into her driveway
and how he
wanted to have
two daughters with her

but as her
clothes dictated
this was not
to be

as her religion
confined him
to a place
outside her life

she still had
yet to understand
that some things
run deeper
than what happens
after death

and as friends
relegated messages
between the
two opposing camps

(neither were in
any shape to speak
to each other anymore)

he thought to himself,
"I think I'll have to wait
until my next chance."

Inverted Phallus

if you missed me prove it
wrap those legs around me
let them scream towards the sky
as I whistle joys
between your absinthe soaked thighs

those thighs,
those brutal, hungry, love obvious thighs

religious fanatics have their temples,
their churches, their synagogues,
their Mother Theresa homes for the dying
my place of worship is your g-spot
and what can only be a precious delicacy
as prescribed

much in the same way ice cream was treated
by the rich at the turn of the 19th century
just ask the wife of this nation's
fourth president, Dolly Madison
her favorite ice cream flavor was oyster

some people think that oyster
can be served as an aphrodisiac
I guess we'll have to wait until death
to ask Dolly Madison about that
but hey,
9 out of 10 naked girls can't be wrong

The Seed That Will Grow A Mighty Acorn

the Saki tasted great
especially with her there
and when they left
they lit each
other's cigarettes
and carpooled
with friends
to the show

they were offered
whiskey, which,
with their inclination
of never wanting
to appear rude
they accepted

it was cold out
once they had
reached their destination
he draped his
coat over her
as her friends whispered
what a gentleman he was
and she secretly
desired the jacket

she would get something
akin to it a week later
when shopping

for new clothes

and once inside
the doors
they met more people
some of whom
they didn't know
would be there

in the corner he stood
as she snuck off
to get high

and as the first band's
set ended
he was greeted
by a friend of hers
who told him
how happy she was
that they were together
that she had never
seen Ellie
this happy before
and wanted it
to continue

he didn't
know what to say
other than
to take another drink
of beer

she made him
happy too

and when the headlining
band came on
she returned to his side
even as he danced
with another girl
he had known
since having worked
at the mall

and as she left
to get another drink
she felt a rumbling
in her stomach

she had overdone
it once again

and she wasn't looking
forward to spending
the rest of the show
hunched over
the seat of a toilet
in the women's restroom
as her friends led
her to a stall

where she
could do

exactly that

when she stepped out
the band was just finishing
their set

but he was also standing there
he was too worried
about her
to enjoy the show

"Have you been here the whole time?"
she looked at him

"I have,"
he nodded
as he put his
coat over her

"But you missed your band."

"This is my third time seeing them,"
he said, putting an arm
around her
as she laid her head
on his shoulder
and they left
the venue

Pensive Chivalry

the light on the porch flickered
he knew his roommate
would never fix it

there were walls upstairs
that had been torn down
but never replaced too

but that's how things were here

an ambulance and fire truck drove by

there was always an
ambulance and fire truck driving by

cops too

and the for-hire security agency
that the rich people
down the street paid for
but he didn't mind
it just meant
there would be fewer
nights during the summer
when his neighbors could be heard
shouting at each other

the house was old
and the walls were thick

you couldn't hear anyone
having sex through these walls

yet for some reason you
could hear the neighbors yelling
at each other during the summer

he liked where he lived
he liked his roommate
and the fact that there
were always people over
and something going on
he liked that he lived next to
where everything went on
in town

that didn't always mean
he was up for doing something
though

sometimes, he had to remind
himself of that

Sew All the Words, Reap the Benefits

"Let's enter a poetry contest,"
she said, looking up from her phone

"I didn't know you wrote,"
he replied, turning from the coffeemaker

"Just a little here and there."
she got up from her chair
to retrieve a notebook
from the living room
and set it in front of him
on the kitchen counter

"See?"

he flipped through its pages
and one line
jumped out at him:
"but you were keeping me safe
in the back of your mind"

"That poem's what I think of you,"
she smiled, lighting a cigarette

"It's what I was always meant to do,"
he thought, as he dropped what he was doing
and put her cigarette out
before walking her
to bed

Deleterious

there was so much loneliness
in the room
that it could sink a battleship

tapping the remaining
tobacco out from its place
in the rod
he set it in the ashtray

the computer screen
was on
it was the only source
of light right now

and he sat
at the edge of the bed
wondering
what to type next

Swarming In Viscera

she decried
the word "afterbirth"
for her it was too much

just the idea
of all those organs inside
once being necessary
to sustaining a human life
all of a sudden becoming unnecessary

to her there was
something wrong
about that

and she shuddered
at the thought
of someone fishing around
the inside of her guts
to pull those organs out

the blood, the fluids

all of it a reminder
of a smaller place
yet inside

In Tandem

turning off the lights
they sat naked
from each other

neither had expected
for this to happen

they hadn't even planned
on speaking again

but they were both here
now

he noticed how
even in the dark
her smile brought
out the dimples
of her face

and the way she looked
at him
was one of quiet contentment

she had made it
after all

their limbs had
been wrapped around each
other for so much

of the night

but now was their time

to be how they never
had the chance to be
before

and as she traced
the scar on his face

with her finger
she thought of all the other
men and places
she had been

and how he looked at her
and called her home

Spontaneous Piece of Human Flesh

they stood in the corner
him and his friend
it was Halloween
and true to form
they were the only ones
not in costume

but they had their name tags
with his reading "Holland,"
and his friend's reading "Denmark"

no one questioned
nor were they interested
in the joke

band after band performed
they were all garage bands
or heavy metal acts
the type you see
with alarming frequency
in central Illinois

but as the night went on
they gravitated
towards one another
them and the others
they knew

it turns out

they were all spread
throughout different rooms
of the frat house

all these people
who knew each other after all
it was so much easier
being together
after that

and as the night continued
NPR played old blues
and country string standards
from the nineteen twenties and thirties
Denmark found a girl
he was interested in
someone he had seen
at shows before
but whom he had
failed to talk to

they started talking
which led to kissing
and fondling beneath a blanket
on the couch
in front of a group
of at least twenty people
who promptly
vacated the room

Holland didn't though

and as they got more intimate
beneath the blanket
Holland lifted it
to snap shots of their hands
covering body parts
in various states of arousal
as the people he knew
snickered in the background

and when he finished
he met with an Asian girl
who was sitting in the dining room
and playing a song on a piano
that she had supposedly heard
from an old Italian film
she had seen when she was young

but she wasn't young anymore

and when the night ended
Holland left with the Asian girl's
phone number

it turned out her name was Sarah

and he left Denmark lying there
on the couch, spent,
with a one night stand to remember

The Happenings At 327 Maple Leaf

she could pack
what he had given her away
but she couldn't
change that they'd
had sex in nearly
every room of the house

nor could she escape
how he was the first thing
she thought about
any time she tried
using his cuffs and chains
on a different person

his presence
was still very much felt

her dog would even jar and wake
each time a truck that
sounded like his
would drive by
and there were times
he wouldn't even respond
to her calling him
instead he would just sit
and look out the window
for the man who used to spend
so much time there to reappear

he never did

getting up to go to work
she saw the toothbrush he had left
in the medicine cabinet
and she remembered a time
when she kept their toothbrushes together

she threw it away just before leaving

when she came home
from the gym that night
she showered and readied for bed
but couldn't sleep

needing a way to pass the time
she looked through
one of the manuscripts he had left
and thought how each word
was a part of him

that he was still there

she put the manuscripts back
and took a joint out
to the breezeway
where she sat down, lit up
and thought "*What have I done?*"

Machine Gun Soul

these are the kinds of girls
that will take or find anything
for a distraction:
roll up paper clips, eat generic fruit snacks,
deliberately mail unaddressed envelopes
while spreading venereal disease
beneath apple trees
at 4:00 in the afternoon

and if you want something from them
don't bother asking
because they will give it to you
just out of distraction

but at the same time
they'll find themselves
not wanting to look at you
because the time you fisted them
felt too great
and it reminds them of a place
they'll never know
a machine gun soul

rabid, fiery, penis hungry, snot consuming
gouging out
bullet after bullet after precious bullet

if they had eyes
they would have purchased a cruise ship

and exploded, long ago

a miniature tadpole
a pebble falling into the water
flowers opening in the rain
and mangos over-ripening
in grocery store fruit stands
these girls' cunts know everything
and are familiar
with knowing what they have isn't there

but it's not a distraction

the last game of chess won
by a king being placed next to a bishop
the next terrorist attack
what's inside these girls
is all just probable and eventual

"Please pass the salt."
calendars bought
and days long since past
advocating the time
since you were there

just ask D.W. Dwayne Hausser
communist, children's book author
he who was very much so there
and felt very much the same way
feeding himself
on lust, razors, coffee and coffin nails

just so he could be sure
that he was leading
the most uncomfortable life
imaginable . . .

. . . and he did . . .

light shows
the kind at rock shows
put on by bands
that sadly, have not released
new collective material
since the nineteen seventies

and life
will be coming out
between these girls' legs
oozed in distraction

Susurrations

spelling his name
phonetically
for all the nice people

it still didn't matter

but he thought
how nice
it was
to have no one
paying attention

and how this took
as much effort
as sitting on
her couch
watching TV

it's what he imagined
her to be doing
right now

leaf in the wind
mud on an untied shoe
looking through a window
trying to drown out
the sounds
of more pious spirits

Fugue

I took one last look
at her tiny furniture
and was gone

there was nothing else to do

so I stopped by a friend's
and drank too much wine
while his dog looked at me
and I lamented
on what I had lost

again

it seemed that three months
was the breaking point
after that
there was no point to carry on

I didn't know if it was something I did

but the girls tired of me quickly

and every time
I thought I had finally worked things out
I was told how a punch
to the back of the head
was preferred
as opposed to a back massage

or a quiet evening at home
smoking a hookah

we stayed up that night
my friend and I
listening to old reggae 45s
and talking about community college

and as the sun came up
I thought how I had done this with her
hundreds of times

*

he looked
at the person's face
as they blew into
the harmonica
and thought how
the facial expression
they made
must resemble
that of an ass blowing
out a beer shit
scattershot
into the toilet

and he felt a little
better after that
walking to the
bathroom
to relieve himself
of all the coffee
he had drank

Posthumously

the most natural course of existence
is that it ends
the most unnatural course of existence
is living forever

I've never heard of anything doing that
living forever
not a lichen, not a bacteria, not a war,
not vampires, not highlanders,
not Penn & Teller
and definitely not the turtle
that was discovered
a few years back
that had a musket ball stuck in its shell
that dated back
from the American Revolutionary War
that turtle to, will die someday

things conclude, life concludes
and I've never seen any proof
of anything supernatural
ever occurring or being in existence

they say you need faith to believe in God
but I think that faith
is just an earmark of ignorance
the simple truth
that needs to be said is this:
we're all somewhat

the slightest bit uncomfortable
with our own mortality
so what seems the logical step
in curing that fear
is convincing ourselves
that we'll live forever
someplace else

the same way I could live forever
if I moved to Miami,
or the Las Vegas that's in Ohio
but I probably wouldn't live forever
if I'd move to either of those spots
much the same way
you wouldn't live forever
if there actually was a place called heaven
but the chances are
that I probably would get laid a lot
(in heaven)

Her Electrical Corset

he never understood
the manner
in which she saw
herself

when he looked at her
he saw a complete young woman
who looked even better
when she wasn't wearing makeup
and had her hair tied back
while wearing a spaghetti strapped shirt
and looking at him with wide open eyes
as he stopped by her place
to give back her phone
at two in the morning

or how she stood
in the doorway
and wore only a towel
before opening it
liberally to him
as he took a three hour break
to visit her
from work

they had much to discuss
that afternoon
and the first of those matters
was how that towel

just had to go
and he was glad
she so willingly complied

but she just
didn't see herself
in the same light
as he did

instead she saw herself
riddled with bullet holes
not because they
were actually there
but because that's how
she had been conditioned
from previous boyfriends
to see herself
and how she didn't want
to disappoint

but he liked the
steak fajitas that she cooked
and how she posted
a picture of them online
above a statement
proudly declaring
that she knew how to treat her man right

and she did too

but he didn't know

what he had done
to deserve
what she was
putting him through now

why she wanted
to be alone
especially after having
been with the other men
that she had

or how every time
he checked his phone
he did it with
the subconscious thought
that it might be her
calling or texting

even though
he knew it wouldn't be

Vignette

they saw one another
at the bar
and neither
could remember
when they had spoken last

so he wrote her an email
with the hope of reconnecting

a few months passed
and she responded
saying she wanted
to talk as soon as possible

when he texted
she said she was eating
but to give her a call
in a half-hour

then he had printer problems
and wasn't able to call on time

when they finally did speak
it was like they had
never stopped

the conversation
came easy
to them

there was something
natural in the connection
they shared

when he asked
if she was seeing anyone
she said no
that she had just left
a bad relationship
where she was abused

he said he was sorry
it was something
he hadn't known
and she confessed
that all of the men
she had been with
were like that

he asked her why
and she said
she didn't know

it was her stock answer
one she used quite often

they continued talking
and they opened up
about things
neither had ever
spoken of before

such as his predilection
for handcuffs and lollipops
and her wanting to be tied to a chair

they worked out an arrangement
to meet that Wednesday

as the days passed
it seemed like they were
always together

calling and texting
or sneaking dirty pictures
when the time permitted

eventually the night came
and they met for dinner
but she was running late

it was alright
it would give him a head start
on his meal
so he could take her
back to his place
all that much sooner

when she finally came
she commented that she
didn't like how the waitress
was flirting with him
or how a girl

at another table
was checking him out

he told her that she made
all other women unnecessary
and paid their bill

they went back to his house
where she parked
and followed him in

opening the door he began to say
"This is my kitchen-"

before he could finish
she was on top of him
as he shut the door
and seven years of lust
finally started
to work its way
out from their bodies

Small Solace

poems can feel
like a hollow victory

they won't bring
her and I back

they can't even
bring back
tomorrow

they can however
attract the attention
of a barista with
a phenomenal posterior
that jettisons further out
than most

and whose pants
are having a hard time
keeping those cheeks in check

it nearly looks
like they could spill out
and start
their own continent

and as she sits
listening to his poem
she'll think of

going to the bathroom later
and wondering
if it were possible
that he
could write a poem
about her

Ascendant

he sat on the couch
as she made hot chocolate
in the kitchen
they had just settled in for the evening
after deciding to watch
a slasher film from the 1980s

as he rested his head back
he thought how every place
felt like home when she was around
whether they were dealing
with belligerent employees
at fast food restaurants
or handcuffing each other to a chair
or calling each other a "Christian"
or an "Atheist"
whenever she was around
he knew there was no
other place he'd rather be

as she walked into
the living room
a mug of hot chocolate
in each hand
he prepared to feel
her body brace against his
as he picked up the remote
to turn the movie on

wantingly, her dog looked at them
as they settled next to each other
prepared to enjoy
another perfect evening

She's Omni

it's all together something more lustful
than staying up reading Bukowski
late at night
while hearing Terry Zwigoff movies
play in the whirlwind background

one of the film's characters
is discussing gay tennis players
from the nineteen thirties

true story
as I smoke my cigarette
and no, not that something cigarette
you altogether disgusting pervert
although that many a more girl has choked
and not smoked upon it

my disgusting fluids
flowing down their throats
making them one, turning them whole
into some sort
of anticlimactic raptured beast
my altogether and whole raptured beast
and caged into something
far less significant
and sometimes maybe not

sometimes my being me
rests upon my being Mexican

although sometimes together maybe not
depending on what mood
I attempt to be upon

but my thoughts and memories turn to her
the girl in the otherwise
empty, swollen pink jacket
unless her form has more to say
as something epic spindle fibers undone
and this way comes

late on a Monday night
while reading Bukowski on my bed
smoking a cigarette
and once again thinking of her
the girl in the pink jacket

I dream of filling her crevasses
and turning her into
my own piece of art
I want my love jammed up her cunt
fiercely and neurotic, independent,
silent, like her eyes
protected beneath her horned,
thick rimmed glasses

unveiled, slight
in the sight you'll never see,
before or again

unlike the gaze invited upon you

from the eyes of some avid pot smoking
or cigarette addicted frenzied little girl
who knows nothing about life

not my cigarette addiction though
but altogether, once and again
something else

I've never felt this way before

A Crisis of Confidence

he knew
she'd never stop
complaining

it was in her blood

like an astronaut
hitting golf balls
on the moon

and as he listened
to her
over the phone
he thought
how you don't
always get
to choose
who ends up
in your life

Opaque Glass

she lives
like an Ingmar Bergman film
a pronounced silence
fell between her words

the way she moved
between frames
was one of
elegance and grace
a regal presence
unique only to her

yet when she spoke
it was only
to announce
what she didn’t mean

and what
she was thinking
at that precise moment
she never knew

she was accustomed
to living like this
it was the only way
she had ever known

but she
had her camera

and her film
and she preferred
to take her pictures
in black and white

it was always
so much easier
to discern
the forms
that way

and the presence
which she felt
was always there

Eros, Baby

no more are the days
a cup of coffee in one hand
a lovely lady's
in the other

fortunately, I still get
the coffee for free though

and the girl's hand
was always best attached
to an arm, which in turn
was connected
to a living, breathing, warm ass body

I'm not a murderer
or anything of the like

I also seriously doubt
though the evidence
might point to the contrary
that I would have the guts
to cut someone's arm off

that could be a good thing
to be considered though

it's this type of situation
that makes me think
"*Have the girls that I've been with*

seriously liked me for me
or the part of me that is a writer?"

it reminds me
of the last girl I was with
her skin
was an illustrious pale
her hair, a peppermint red
her eyes, a mint green

the girl's figure
was svelte beyond belief:
trim, fit, Goodness Goddess,
she was just a miniature
I could have snapped her in half
doing what we did

only after she asked me to read
campfire stories and poetry to her
did she demand, "Fuck me."

it was during the act
that she told me,
"You fuck like you write,"
and that confounded me
I guess I'm just simply good at both
I've certainly had
a lot of practice with both

but now, the weakness is creeping in
and sex is simply

all any girl that I've ever met wants
not to say that's a bad thing
sex is what keeps the human race going

well, okay
maybe sex can be interpreted
as a bad thing

The Girl We Know That We Don't Know

she is everywhere
on everyone's minds
on their Facebook pages
and should you friend her
you'll receive a plethora
of emails from people
you don't know asking,
"How do you know her?"

the fliers for her rock band
are posted everywhere
but mostly on the walls
of the bars
where she'll be performing

soon her fingers
will be tapping and holding
down the keys of the keyboard
she'll be playing
as her band is both
performing and recording
to a room full of bar flies
some of whom won't even care
if she's there
some of whom won't even
know that she's around
but some of whom will feel fortunate
enough to bask in her presence

and as the music plays
and the coffee brews
he'll be standing there
in the back of the room
complimenting on her hair
to his friends endlessly

but he'd never speak to her
or tell her that face to face
because that would take
too much effort on his part
and he wouldn't want to break
his perfect record of refusing
to bat an eye
even if that would benefit him socially
no, not for one second

so he chooses to go on
standing there in the dark
and feel invincible
due to his continued anonymity
as another Saturday night
slowly passes by

37 Days After the Incident Happened

the priest looked at him
he was stone faced and weary eyed
"How can I help you?"

he explained why he was there

"That doesn't make any sense,"
the priest folded his arms
across his chest
"If she was a practicing Christian,
then it'd make sense."

he didn't have the heart to mention
her bandwagon lesbianism

"Let me get you some literature."
the priest stood and walked
to the cabinets
with his papers in them

"Since you haven't
had a Catholic upbringing
there is much to go over."
he thumbed through his files
and closed the cabinet
before taking a seat
at his desk

"If you don't mind me saying,

you seem pretty rooted in your disbelief.
I don't exactly know how I can help you."

he had prayed for her twice
each time during a difficult time
in her life
and he was wanting to see
if there was a more spiritual side
to himself
one that he didn't know about

the priest shook his head
"Are you doing this for her?"

he said he didn't know

"Give me your address,"
the priest reached for a pen and paper

he said his address
and could feel a relief
on the priest's part
that he would be gone soon

"I'll send you what I can find
through the mail."
the priest sat back in his chair
"After that we could set up a meeting
if you'd like."

he thanked the priest for his time

and got up to leave

on the way out
the priest told him
not to confuse the supply closet
for the exit

it was something
he had done
literally dozens of times

An Impending Frigid Moment

"I'm not going to answer my phone,"
she told him
"The only reason I'd have for answering it
is right here."

they hadn't done much that day
other than sleep, dodge phone calls
and eat breakfast
they hadn't even had sex yet

they were watching a movie
with the commentary on
and the slow, dull voice
of the director
was betraying the sense
of comic relief he was providing
by talking about the woman
in the leading role
and how she was selected
because she was the only woman he knew
willing to take her top off

as they watched the movie
he turned to her
to see her eyes
start to close
as her mind
slowly drifted into sleep

he'd never known anyone
who slept as much as her
but he didn't mind
it gave him the chance
to be with his favorite person
and the chance to write and be alone

taking his laptop out
he thought
of the perfect way
of waking her
an hour or two
from now

by spreading her legs apart
and opening her pants
and pressing a cube of ice
against her clit

he knew she'd like that

Flailing

breathing the
language
was never
enough

he had to
stab his way
through it
in a better
attempt
to master
it

his life

he tried his
best to get
an understanding
but was told
that the way
he viewed things
was a constant
misrepresentation

he didn't know
what he could
do anymore

he could

light a cigarette
or open
a dictionary
to see if
there was
something he had
missed

and perhaps there was

but exasperation
was getting
the better
of him

he thought
back to footage
he had seen
of sea tortoises
that had been blinded
by the radiation
they were exposed to
at Bikini Atoll

and how he envied
them

their trial
would be over
soon enough

their skeletons
would soon
litter the beaches
where they
had drawn
their last breath

a celebration of life
in all its darkest
forms

Kingdom of Open Limbs

he wasn't expecting this

people stretched out
everywhere

this was a bar after all
and not the house
of one of the girls
he had known
several years back

stepping into a room
he saw his friend
sitting at a booth
with a girl whose face
disappeared into his lap

despite the music
he could still hear the sounds
and he thought
how they were the most depressing
things he had ever heard

no matter where he stepped
a similar picture
was painted everywhere
until a girl came up
and asked him
what was up

he honestly didn't know anymore

all he wanted was a cigarette
and reaching for his pocket
he discovered her hand
already waiting there

taking it he led her outside

"She's nice," he thought
with how her conversation
tended to gravitate towards
how Brueghel dropped
the "h" from his name

as he stood in the street
contemplating his past
he saw a couple pass by
the girl was upset
and the guy was struggling
to keep up by telling
her how sorry he was
that he didn't mean
to fool around with that other girl

and he thought to himself
how the night was now complete
how any time that he had ever gone out
he saw a couple fighting in the street
proving to himself
that he was finally there

People Being Murdered All the Time

when she turned to me
and said,
"I don't want to die tonight."
I replied,
"Then don't."

we then made
the closest thing to love
I've ever made

A Face Full of Mountains

the deer flew
through my windshield
late at night

I was almost immediately rushed
to the hospital
when the paramedics arrived
they had to find me first
apparently I was stumbling
around a cornfield
with glass and deer guts
all over my face

my first memory
when I reached the hospital
was my mom standing over me
and talking
I couldn't see her though
my eyes refused to open

someone, a nurse
was talking to her
she had a very dusky voice

"She sounds hot,"
I said to no one in particular
to which I promptly received
no reply

just before my surgery a priest
arrived to pray for the best
"I won't be needing any of that,"
I told him
"But they might."
I pointed to my family
I had partially regained my vision
by that point

during the surgery the doctors placed
a metal plate on the right temple
of my skull
which was fractured
(to this day I have yet to go through
a metal detector at an airport to see
if it would go off)

when I woke up post surgery
my throat felt like it was full of glass
but at least my TV was turned to MSNBC
this was back when Keith Olbermann
was still on

I couldn't look at my face
for days after the accident
according to me I didn't have one

but when I finally gathered the courage to
I was in a room without a mirror
so I took a picture on a camera phone

what I saw was a picture of
the same person more or less

the parts of my face not cut away
were a bruised and purpled
mountain range
and there was this deep chasm cut across
the center of my face that to this day
I call the "Grand Canyon"
(some people think they look like
cat whiskers)

not that I let any of this get to me
I still carried on with my life
more or less
I even attended a concert up in Chicago
a few nights later where I met a girl
and continued the time honored tradition
of failing to get her phone number

my one regret about
the whole ordeal is that I wasn't able
to save the deer's head to have it
it stuffed and mounted
scavengers got to that

but then you'll have that

Abstart

I was waiting for my paycheck
when a girl
I've told myself
not to like anymore
walked up
and fixed the collar
of the dress shirt
I was wearing
just beneath my suit jacket

I had no tie on that day

normally her bangs hung frustrated
above her forehead
I'd brush them off to the side for her
but today
they were perfectly arranged
and in order

we looked at each other
the author and the artist
before taking our paychecks
and leaving

Abdication

I'm sad to hear
that you'd rather me tell you stories
instead of experiencing them with me
first hand

you were always anxious like that

I see that you got your nose pierced
and dyed your hair differently
since the time I saw you last
it was black and white before
now it's three shades of brunette

I don't pretend to understand you
or know where you're coming from
it's just that to me
you've always seemed unhappy

a friend once made the remark
"You can always tell when a girl
has just broken up with a boyfriend.
She will change something
about herself physically
to reflect the changes
she is going through psychologically."

"To reinvent herself as it were."

all I can say

is that you must always
be going through
something psychological

I lost interest in talking to you
about halfway through our dinner
after you explained to me
the mechanics of our friendship
"You talk and I listen."

there's something sad in that
usually I like to hear
what's happening in the lives
of those dear to me

apparently, you are not

Tess

she wasn't like
the other girls
he'd seen
that night

she was dressed
in a polyester button up
she had found
second hand
and had dress slacks
she had altered
into bell bottoms

her fair skin
complimented her
auburn hair
well enough
that he wondered
what she looked
like naked

he went to
talk to her
but she wasn't interested
in what he had
to say

it was the gel
in his hair

she liked natural

ironically, so did he
and nothing seemed
more natural than putting
that gel in his hair
every morning
even though
it was out of style

that's what attracted him
to her
that they
were the two
most out of style
people in the room

that didn't mean
however
she wasn't
without her preferences

Fluffer

I fall before your goddess cunt
like a monk who's taken a vow of silence

only my tongue is free
to do whatever it wants

Her & All Her Stupid Mistakes

her mom
didn't approve
which meant
she would
follow
through
with it

and her
friends were
no longer
there
to sustain
her
which meant
she had
lost the
confidence
from others
which she so
naturally
lacked

and she
had made
sure to be
as unpleasant
as possible
to him

as to ensure
the one person
who believed
in her
would never
go out
of his way
to contact
her again

she was
fine with this
she took
comfort in it
she derived
a strength
from it

but it wasn't
the type
of strength
familiar
to others

it was
a strength
in codependency
knowing that
she would
be the only one
doing all the work

it was a sadness
that brought
out the worst
in her
a craving
for mistreatment
and inconvenience

she had
gone out of
her way
to do this
to herself
and to others
yet again

she knew not
why she did this

it was a question
she never thought
of asking herself

and there
was simply
no turning back

Old Man

I am an old man: epic, titanic, moon shot
these feet have walked
across thousands of miles
some of which no longer exist

this skin could very well
outlast the parchment
that the Declaration of Independence
is written on
this skin sure does feel like the parchment
that the Declaration of Independence
is written on
and if properly preserved,
at least for novelty's sake
this skin might very well
outlast the very nation
that the Declaration of Independence
represents

that is if George W. Bush
has anything to say about it

I have been with many women:
countless, listless, thankless,
the latest having been my wife of 27 years
she's been dead the past eight

much like the way they stormed
the beaches of Normandy

or the way a man is confined
to his wheelchair
or the way quarks are connected
to make a proton
all things come to an end

I no longer have a family,
I no longer have any point
of getting out of bed in the morning
I lost that when I retired
from the post office
five years ago

I'm my very own
one hundred fifty degree angle

I still collect a pension;
lifetime security insured
by the government
from their government job
your tax dollars are going to support me
the benefits of selected socialism

I knew there was a reason
I voted Democratic

but it's enough to pay
for my daily cup of coffee and cigarettes
and buy some time
with my crossword puzzle
every damn day

. . . varicose veins are everywhere . . .

the celebrated atheist Sam Harris
once wrote a book
trying to defeat the theory of free will
somebody has proven him wrong
at least once now
who has a body
that would want to live this long?

Well Spoken Soft Spoken

he looked at her
and wondered
what it meant
to be well adjusted

not that
he imagined
that she knew
she just looked
the part

sitting there
giving scathing
reviews for books
she had read in class

the way she
held her coffee
with just the tips
of her thumb
and index finger
indicated some
sort of strength
in her hands
at least

he didn't know
if that strength
would extend

to her mind
but she at least
felt comfortable
enough discussing
the works
of postmodernists
even if she
didn't agree
with the aim
of their work

he liked hearing her speak
there was a cadence
to the flow of her words
and every conversation
felt like spoken word poetry

confirming to him
what he already suspected
that she had
a basic understanding
and appreciation
of how to construct
a sentence

and that she would always
be available to talk to him
even if her words weren't

Prepping the Talons She Wished She Had

she said how she wanted new clothes
and tattoos
like he was holding
her back

that's when he began to think
there must be something else
if that's the best
she could come up with

so they talked some more
and she divulged
that he wasn't the type
she was interested in

"So what attracted
you to me
in the first place?"
he asked
to which he
received no reply

but the more
they spoke
the less
things made sense

she said his not believing in God
would mean

that he wouldn't
go to church
with her
and their
future daughters

"You have no idea
what I would do for you,"
he said

she thought of the things that
he had done
and how right he was by telling her this
that she didn't know what else
he would be willing
to do for her

but for now
all that she wanted
was for him
to pack his things
and leave

Not Proper Discussion for Dinner Time with Your Family

between the two of them
they only had fifty six years
but they had come to a point
in their relationship
where she didn't just
feel comfortable
but enjoyed
going to the bathroom
in front of him
so much so
that she bragged
about it to her mom
at dinner

she loved playing
the part of most complete family member
at her gatherings
so much that she reminded
her uncle of the time
he came over
to drop off the chest of drawers
he had painted for her
only to hear them having sex
in the backroom
of her house

it was her favorite sound
hearing him

inside her

her boyfriend
not her uncle that is

and the feeling
of the sensation
was beyond words

just what orifice
did she have
that he didn't
belong in?

not while there was still
a beat in her heart
or the draw of air in her lungs
that could keep her
from finding a way
of giving him everything
he always wanted

Something Else Happened

they spoke on the phone
and when she asked
what happened
he said he didn't know

that's why he was calling her

she explained that women
in abusive relationships
can generally go back
to their abuser seven times

at that point
they either stop
or are dead

he didn't know
if that was the case
but he was open
to suggestions

she said she'd be willing
to pick up some pamphlets
from the local women's abuse center
and that she could get them
to him the next time
they'd see each other
a week from now

he thanked her

he was grateful that someone
was willing to lend
an open ear
to his paranoia

Handsome Young Poem

when we'd meet up
after getting off our jobs
I'd be tired
and she'd smell like coffee
"I brought you some coffee
to make for us tonight,"
her voice sounded like silk

though I think that would
be a bit uncomfortable
for her physically
if she had actual silk
coming out of her mouth

we'd go back to my place
(meaning my parent's house)
and there I would grind
Irish cream coffee beans
and mix them with whiskey
to make Irish coffee

for a vegetarian
meaning she was supposed
to have a weak stomach
she sure could gulp that shit down

she'd pick out a movie
while I tried to get some writing done
she would then proceed to watch

movie after movie
after unbreakable movie
she would watch them
like she would take sleeping pills

all the while
I never felt the tremendous need
to impress her
all I had to be
was all I ever was
the author and the coffee drinker

this perfect little person
usually fell asleep by herself
toes curled up
not beneath the blanket
and just a little bit drunk
in the middle of the night
on my bed
shit like that's just not fair

I don't pretend
or make excuses
that bed she slept on
was the only one in the room
but I knew
that I didn't want to
treat her like all the others

the other girls . . .

so I'd go to sleep
at the far end of the bed
for what good that did
we'd usually wake up
body to body, fully clothed
and the both of us
late for work

one morning
on January 1st when we woke up together
I tried kissing her
but when she pulled back
I playfully asked,
"You know this takes two people?"

clearly I was no match
for New York City
you'll always lose the girl
to New York City
she never did
move to New York City

we didn't hang out much after that
I did find out however
much later on
that she made an appearance
in a screenplay turned novel
extravaganza

Just Sitting By

"You're lucky," he said
"You don't have to put up with women."

"Don't I?" his friend
who was gay responded
as they laughed

it was something easy to do
particularly since they had known
each other since grade school

but they were sitting there now
in the throes of middle age
and with the exception
of bills, jobs, houses
and writing
they hadn't changed much
that they were always
what each other had
along with a TV show,
a beer in their hands
and a yard
where they could sit
and watch the happenings
at the elderly couple's house
across the street
who weren't
talking anymore

this was their entertainment
for the night
as they had both just come
out of relationships
they wished they still had

but each understood
their predicament
that these things
come and go
like the paint
they had used earlier
on one of the new doors
that they purchased
with an 11% discount

Never Wear Your Heart on Your Sleeve During a Knife Fight

writing a poem
and as the pen
bleeds black blots
all over the paper
I'm stuck with the memory of you
your hair, your tattoos,
the ugly lamp in your living room,
your dog, our chair,
the Christmas tree
my grandmother gave you
which I helped set up,
the cinema sign
you got me that Christmas,
the coffee cans we used
to put our cigarettes out in
and how it hurt more than
any deer flying through
the windshield of my car ever could
when you said you didn't
want to be together anymore
and I think to myself
"*What a great three months.*"

Replete With Beverages

neither had accents
they were both from the Midwest

but he knew
she was looking
out for him
in her own way
whenever
she brought a twelve pack
of beer or soda home

he'd reward her
by taking off her shirt
in the kitchen
and she would smile
that it was so nice
having someone
to come home to

she called him
one of her two boys
the other being the dog
she had rescued
from a shelter

he had been found
protecting a litter
of kittens
whose mother had died

as they settled in
she whispered don't ever leave

to him
not the dog
that is

and he pledged that
he never would
his face lost in her breasts
they were double Js

"Good," she tilted back her head
"I look forward to making coffee
for you in the morning."

Insurmountable

except for all the blood
he thought women were beautiful
on their periods
how they would over analyze things
and completely cave
to their hormones
and let every tiny suspicion, truth
and untruth escape, sink in

how they would decimate
relationships on a whim
knowing they could be replaced
with someone else

he wondered what it would be like
to be capable of something like that
to be completely selfish
and let your insecurities run free

but he never had to put up with that

the most he had to put up with
were finding the words to put on the page

but he had been the cause
for the blood
on at least one occasion

being intimate with her

he had gone too far
and that's when he felt
something thicker
then her natural lubricant
begin to coat him

and when he pulled out
he saw his reward
staining both him
and the bed

they retreated to the bathroom
where they cleaned themselves
and she said,
"This is the last time I ever
let you do that to me."

Delicatessen

it was three in the morning
I was sitting in the basement
writing on politics, pancakes,
when she came through
the cellar door

her theme
offered me a glance
while her black hair
reminded me of water
stained from coffee grounds

she shut the door behind her

her dress hung from her
loose bound
on it was a floral print
while forest green colored the background

delicate, delightful
near as I could tell
that dress was ready
to fall to the ground

I wanted it to

I knew what lay beneath
and between
those legs . . .

wet, hairy, fun
tinged with a mint flavor
just between my tongue
and the air

licorice, red lips and those eyes
waiting
behind thick rimmed glasses
they look up to the sky
and only
belong to me
the show that is on
only for me

. . . my sweet delicatessen . . .

Clarion Call

he cinched his tie
and put on a sweater
he was readying
for another day
without her

he drank his coffee
and smoked
a cigarette
the news was
on TV
but he wasn't
watching

checking his cell
he saw he had
two text messages

the first was from
his father
who wished
him a good day

the second
was from a girl
he had met
during the weekend
saying she had
a good time

and she hoped
to see him again
soon

he thought
the same thing

how it was nice
to come out
from his cycle
at least once
in a while
and that she
represented
the chance
for something
new again

he texted her
that he was
going to work
now
but that he
could call
when he
was off

it only took
a moment
for her
to respond

"Most def."

he didn't
have the charm
of the wandering
drug addicts
she was used to
but he was honest
and he wrote
which was something

it was a start

and the both
of them would think
throughout the span
of the day
just how this evening's
conversation
would go

Androgynous Strip

sexless, shapeless
the hordes came
filtering in
to their feel good time party

they were
remorseless
not knowing
what they did

it didn't matter
just as long
as time passed

the hands of a clock
unburdened by
their desires

amorous

slowly thinking
taking time
to drink
all things in

Her Sinister Strands

there was something
sinister in the way
she grasped
at straws
trying to find
the reason for
his not being
needed anymore

it didn't matter
that she believed in what
she was saying
as much as it sounded
like she did

and that caused problems

she wanted a clean slate
a fresh start

but when she actually
heard herself
she knew
that the seeds of doubt
had already been planted
from within

and as she would post online
for some time
after that

how hard it was
with moving on

even though she had
initiated the incident herself

that no matter
how many times
she dyed her hair
afterwards
the thought
would always be there
gnawing
at her roots

Storyboard Collection

here on Earth
people spend their time
driving, reading, writing books, prose,
voting, smoking cigarettes,
having sex, being violent, listless or boring,
drinking, suicide bombing,
product placement advertising

eating steaks,
being vegan, vegetarian, vagitarian,
relaxing, smoking grass,
passing up on opportunity
giving in to chance
drinking coffee, making movies, debating,
standing around at parties,
waiting for somebody to talk to them

. . . waiting . . .

moving, going, leaving, gone
(being away from home)
taking pictures, hammering,
raving, dancing,
criticizing . . .

. . . democratizing . . . ?

working, wearing clothes,
wearing black,

manufacturing, traveling, packing,
bringing lunch to significant others,
making fun of George Bush,
(not something hard to do)
giving birth to babies . . .

. . . there are always babies being born . . .

performing music,
giving lectures, dying,
listening or reading this

Don't Take Your Cue From This

she was watching
videos of public officials
killing themselves
on live TV
and wondered
how they did it

she knew how
they did it
with their fingers
on the trigger

but she wondered
what shame or humility
could make a person
write their own
exit

she had experienced
problems before

neglect, being locked
in a closet by an
abusive significant other,
her parent's divorce,
she was committed
to the psych ward
of a hospital for awhile

even then
deep down
she knew she didn’t
have what it took
to write her
own exit

Viced

when he entered the bedroom
she looked up from her book
to watch him undo his shirt
two buttons at a time

she liked that
it meant she could
rest her head against
his bare chest
and listen to his heart beat
that much sooner

and as he joined her
beneath the covers
her fair figure welcomed
him with its warmth
and open limbs

when they had finished
she laid her head on his chest
and listened to his heart flutter
as she felt the fluids he had left inside
start to settle

her pills would insure
they wouldn't survive the night

it was enough to remind her
of a conversation they once had

about when life starts
she said it begins at conception
while he said it begins
when the sperm and egg
come into existence
even before they are joined in the womb

she had never thought of it like that
and it made her uncomfortable
she had never thought that millions
of potential people were paying the price
for her own personal pleasure

their talk had left her
with much to consider
and as she watched him drift into sleep
she wondered how she could be with
someone who held such a view

it was bad enough she knew he didn't
share her religious beliefs
that had been made clear
when they first met
and she thought how difficult it would be
to have children with him and raise them
in the church the way she wanted to

and he didn't look the way
she felt a man should

just what was it that

she did see in him?

and as she began
to doubt his place in her life
she felt the inside of her thighs
quiver and bleed

she quickly retreated to the bathroom
to clean herself
and take one of the dozen antibiotics
that lined her medicine cabinet

this always happened
when she felt stressed

when she had finished
she came back to the bedroom
where he was already asleep

quietly, she slipped into bed
all but ignoring the drops
of blood she had stained the mattress with
and, pulling the covers over her
turned off the light

she didn't get much sleep though
at least not while his breath was still
on her back
or the weight of his body
on her bed
and she wondered

what it would be like
to fall asleep, for once
with no one else
by her side

For Persephone

so long and whatever's left of goodbye
I'm leaving here, tomorrow, forever

and while you contemplate suicide
and think thoughts you'd rather die
let me do the reassuring girl
in the here and now:
we are what's done and over

the bags have been packed
for the best part of two weeks now
the jobs have been transferred
and the stories have all been told

quite simply put
there are no stories left to unfold

and life waits for me there
along 3500 miles of coastline shore
where the Senator Edmund Muskie
served out his terms

so as my next book
reaches the printed page
or elsewhere
on mass market bookshelves someplace
let me do the reassuring girl:
we are what's done and over

so let us be what we will
with whatever's left of goodbye
my friends are leaving here
tomorrow, forever

Big Heart Dumb Heart

he went to the bar
and ran into
some of her friends

one of them hugged him
and asked how he was doing

he said that he was still adjusting
but that he was doing better

she said she didn't want
to upset him
but she wanted him to know
she had stopped
being friends with Ellie
she had made
a lot of bad choices
since leaving
and that she didn't want to be
a part of that

he said he already knew
though no one had
said it directly to him
but he had a hunch

she said to go with it

it clarified

where he stood
at the moment
other than
the bar

there was nothing
more he could do
and he had
to stop blaming himself
for not saving everyone

he knew her choices
were not his to make

and he wondered
if she ever saw
the error in her thinking
if he would take her back

and the answer
unsettled him

Malevolent Serenade

constant, rhythmic
coming from a place
no one knew

the sounds repeated
there was no
purpose
to them

at least none
that anyone
had discovered
yet

he sat there
listening

it was the only
thing to do

"Why does this exist?"
he wondered
knowing that
if he sat there
it would only
begin again

the sounds were on
a 24 hour loop

every so often
a voice would come on
to read a series
of letters and numbers

codes

he had never heard
the voice though

and if he ever did
he was hoping
that it belonged
to a woman

the frequencies
breathing in
scratching
dropping time
dead

an unseen
obsolescence

if everything else
were to end
he knew
this would persevere

as it always had

seemingly derived from
nowhere
it traveled
a sourceless husk
in and around
everywhere

Epigraph

come, dear, it's getting late
and we wouldn't want
to overstay our welcome

we've dined and drank our host
out of house and home,
and smoked too many cigarettes
which, if not in ashtrays,
decorate the living room floor

so let's take our jackets
and not forget to shut the door
on our way out

goodnight and goodbye, Mr. Vonnegut,
and thank you for all the stories

His Most Depraved Art

armed with an
indefinite supply
of cigarettes
he laid on her bed
typing quietly on his laptop

and when the dog sat up
to leave the room
he knew
what to expect
hearing her car
pull into the drive

immediately, he stopped
what he was writing
saved it
and waited for her
to step into the room

when she did
she greeted him
with her eyes
there was nothing
they could say
to each other
that they couldn't
express with their bodies

as he watched

the way light and shadow
played games between her thighs
as she undressed
he thought how what they had
was incorruptible and insatiable

and how they
would spend the
entire night in bed
only to be interrupted
by a brief stint
of picking up
something to eat
and stopping by the video store
that was going out of business
to see what DVDs
they had for sale

that and the gentle rustling
of her coat being put on
just before leaving
which was enough to ensure
that he'd have an idea
of what to write
poetry wise
tomorrow

It's Just What You Do

going to work
after leaving her place
he passed an elderly couple
on the sidewalk
they were holding hands
and hunched over
walking slowly
as to keep up with each other

he hoped that would
be them someday
after a long life
of taking care
of one another
to still be there
in their final years
doing something as simple
as helping each other
cross the street

taking out his cell phone
he looked at a picture
he had taken of her
and thought she
would always look
that way to him
that she would always
be the young woman
in black

even at an advanced age
with the years
eating away at their bodies
he knew
that nothing would ever take
that away from him
or her

Tangible

not wanting
to expend more energy
than it was worth
he wrote

he wrote until
his eyes
burned red
he wrote until
all the fish disappeared
from the ocean
he wrote
until she was nothing more
than a tombstone

only then
would his job
finally
be complete

December 31st, 2012

she had been looking
forward to it
for some time
so much that he remembered
her mentioning it
as far back
as Thanksgiving

now the time
was upon them
and after lounging
gloriously all day
in their pajamas
they were out and about

he had promised
to take her out
to eat that night
he just didn't know where

reaching a restaurant
that looked suitable
they laughed
as they passed a sign
that read
"sturdy, durable, reliable wigs"

when they entered
the restaurant

they discovered
it was more upscale
on the inside
than it looked
on the outside

when they were seated
the waiter complimented
on their matching
black outfits
and asked
if they had any plans
after this

they answered they did

and when the wine
was brought to them
she mentioned that
she had to tell her mom
about this
that she wouldn't believe
she had found someone
who treated her like a lady

he was glad
to be the one
to do it

they finished their meal
and went to a friend's house

where they were all sitting
in the kitchen
drinking, talking and playing board games

as midnight approached
he lost track of time socializing
while she positioned herself next to him
and even before the clock hand
struck twelve
she kissed him
it's what she had wanted
the last month
and what he had wanted
the last seven years

as the night wore on
more people came and went
but they stayed
lying next to each other on the couch
and as morning approached
they thought how they
could be bringing in the New Year
at home, naked
and turning to one another
saw the same idea
expressed in each other's eyes
before smiling and getting up to leave

Postscript

the cigarettes
didn't offer a taste
anymore

at most they
provided only
a distraction

and as he
left the city
of parking lots
and tattoo parlors
behind
he received a text
from her
wishing him a good trip
and should he need
directions when he
got into town
to give her a call
that she actually
wanted to meet him
before the show

they had only
spoken twice online
a week ago
but he liked her attire
and the band she sang in

and she liked the scar
that ran deep
across his face

she wanted
him to spend
the night
and he needed
the reprieve

and as he texted
that he couldn't
wait to meet
and break in
her new hookah
he thought
how nice
it was
to be needed
if only
for the night

Acknowledgements

The author would like to thank the following for their contributions to Via Storm Clouds: Zach Stein, Cindy Baker, Brittany Vandegraft, Melissa Igwebuike, Nick Bruesch, Vito Vandegraft, Caron Easley, Jessica Stephenson and Lit. on Fire Used Books and you, the reader.